Muffins

FAST AND FANTASTIC

Susan Reimer

CHERRY TREE PUBLICATIONS

Muffins: Fast and Fantastic

Published by Cherry Tree Publications, Edinburgh

Visit themuffinbook.uk

Photography by Caroline Trotter

Design by Alison Rincon

Many thanks also to Lydia, Jamie, Brenda, Jacqueline, Gill, and all my taste testers for their helpful input.

British Library Cataloguing in Publication Data
Data available

ISBN 978 0 9528858 5 6

1st edition 1996; 2nd edition 1999; 3rd edition 2001; 3rd edition revised 2008; 4th edition 2017; 4th edition revised 2020

Printed in the UK by Oxuniprint, part of Oxford University Press

To David, Lydia, and Philip

CONTENTS

INTRODUCTION 4
THE MUFFIN METHOD 6
KNOW YOUR INGREDIENTS 12

Chocolate

Chocolate 18
Chocolate Apricot 21
Chocolate Beetroot 22
Chocolate Cheesecake 24
Chocolate Chip 25
Chocolate Orange 27
Chocolate Pear 28
Chocolate Raspberry 31
Chocolate Ripple 32
Cocoa Courgette 34
Mocha Cheesecake 35
Mocha Cherry 37

Nuts and Oats

Apricot Almond 40
Butter Pecan 43
Cinnamon Swirl 44
Coffee Date 46
Cranberry Oat 47

Fruit 'n' Spice 49
Granola 50
Hazelnut and Chocolate 53
Maple 54
Oat Chocolate Chip 57
Oat Pear 58
Peanut Butter 59

Fruit

Apple Harvest 62
Apple Layer 65
Apple Raspberry 66
Apple Spice 67
Banana 68
Banana Tropical 71
Blueberry 72
Blueberry Cheesecake 75
Butternut Squash (Pumpkin) 76
Carrot Pineapple 79
Gingerbread Apple 80
Lemon 81
Lemon Cheesecake 82
Lemon-Filled 85
Mango 86
Orange 89
Orange Apricot 90

Orange Carrot Spice 93
Peach 94
Pear Ginger 97
Pineapple 98
Plum Orange 101
Raspberry Lemon 102
Raspberry and White Chocolate 105
Rhubarb Almond 106
Strawberry Rhubarb 109

Bran

Apricot Blueberry Bran 112
Orange Date Bran 114
Sultana Bran 115
Yogurt Bran 117

Savoury

Apple and Cheese 120
Cheddar Cheese 123
Feta and Leek 124
Gruyère and Onion 125

THE BASIC MUFFIN 126
GLUTEN- AND WHEAT-FREE 127
SUGAR AND FLOUR NOTES 128

INTRODUCTION

Muffins: Fast and Fantastic has been on a long journey. When it was first published in 1996, American muffins were hardly known in Britain, but people were curious about this new food appearing in cafés. It turned out to be the perfect moment for *Muffins* to come on the scene.

Today, muffins are appearing in all corners of the globe which testifies to their adaptability and appeal. With this global context in mind, I set myself the challenge of updating *Muffins* for a new generation of bakers.

This edition includes 60 recipes plus variations. There is plenty of choice here for everyone. The wide range of batters includes milk, yogurt, buttermilk, sour cream, juice, and purées—combined with a variety of fruits, vegetables, nuts, oats, and chocolate. With the extensive testing that's gone into creating these recipes, I'm confident you're going to enjoy them!

Although the fourth edition was initially written with strong (bread) flour as the flour of choice, I have since decided to revert to plain (cake) flour which is preferred by British bakers. For information about flour conversions and international baking, please see page 128.

Having a background in public health nursing, I'm always keen to promote healthy eating. But having raised a family, I also know the importance of making food that tastes good! The muffins in this book are nutritionally well-balanced with an emphasis on natural flavours and wholesome goodness.

Given our current understanding of fat and sugar, fat no longer takes the blame for many health issues. Dietary fat is essential for maintaining good health but we still want to keep it in balance. Most of these muffins have only 1½ teaspoons vegetable oil or butter per muffin, excluding toppings and fillings.

The World Health Organization recommends restricting sugar consumption to a maximum of 30 grams of 'free' sugar per day for adults. This is about 6 level teaspoons of added sugar. The muffins in this book range from ¼ teaspoon to 2 teaspoons of sugar per muffin (excluding icings). By comparison, most commercial muffins contain 4–5 teaspoons. The sugar content of muffins can be adjusted up or down to suit your preference, so you are in control of the sweetness!

It's worth noting that muffins originated with the common bran muffin, eaten split and buttered as a breakfast quick bread. Muffins are not meant to be as sweet as cake; they are in a category of their own. When keeping the sugar low, you might find that a bit of butter won't go amiss on some of the new flavours too.

For those who are interested in food history, the earliest recorded muffin recipes can be found in late nineteenth century American cookery books, around the time that baking powder was first developed. It wasn't long before recipes spread north to Canada as well. This type of muffin should not be confused with the flat yeast-leavened 'English muffin' which is entirely different and normally served with butter and jam.

Muffins are also part of my own story. During my childhood in the 1960s in Canada, bran muffins were a common snack food in our home. Then, in the 1970s, my mother came across a little book that introduced us to the idea that muffin flavours could extend beyond bran! By the 1980s, muffin-making had become a routine part of my life, baking each week to enjoy fresh, as well as stocking the freezer for snacks and lunch-boxes.

However, after emigrating to the UK with my husband and two small children in 1993, baking became a frustration as my favourite recipes from Canada flopped time and again for no apparent reason. That sparked the beginning of my kitchen experiments and the discovery that British plain flour was significantly different from Canadian all-purpose flour. And so began the *Muffins* story, introducing muffins to the British kitchen.

The technique for making muffins is quick and simple but very different from other forms of baking. To ensure success, please take time to read the following notes about method and ingredients before you begin.

THE MUFFIN METHOD

PREPARATION

All the recipes in this book are designed to produce twelve standard-size muffins although they will reach different heights depending on the ingredients. A standard muffin cup is 5cm across the bottom, 7cm across the top, and 3cm deep. I recommend using paper cases that are at least 3.5cm deep, for optimum rising.

Always read the recipe before you begin, as some require advance preparation. Also it is very important for muffins to bake in a *preheated* oven to achieve correct rising and texture. A large oven will take about 15 minutes to preheat, so always turn on the oven before you begin. Next prepare the muffin tray by inserting paper cases or by greasing with a solid vegetable fat. At this point, you can gather all the ingredients for the recipe and do any special preparation such as chopping and grating.

NOTES ON MEASURING

Accurate measurements are essential for baking, so you will need standardized measuring spoons, a measuring jug, and weigh scales.

All spoon measures are level:

1 tablespoon = 15ml
1 teaspoon = 5ml

Liquid measurements in a jug should be made at eye-level for accuracy. A flexible spatula (bowl scraper) should be used when transferring liquids and batter.

Be careful to use weigh scales for weight measures given in grams (g), and a measuring jug for volume measures given in millilitres (ml).

Although some electronic weigh scales give an option of measuring volume, they are not actually converting weight to volume. They are relying on the fact that many liquid ingredients have matching volume and weight measures, so that 100ml milk weighs 100g, and 50ml juice weighs 50g. However this is not the case for all liquids. For example, 100ml vegetable oil weighs 90g. Having said that, if you understand these principles, then measuring milk and juice on an electronic scale will provide greater accuracy.

As Canadians and Americans normally measure all ingredients by volume, approximate cup measures have been included for dry ingredients. Cup measures for flour and sugar are given on page 128.

MIXING

Each recipe involves making two mixtures: dry and wet. In general, the dry mixture consists of flour, raising agents, and salt. Most of the other ingredients, including sugar, are added to the wet mixture. The dry ingredients should be sifted together to break up any lumps and ensure an even distribution of the raising agents. It's not nice to bite into a lump of raising agent! If you don't have a sieve, use a fork to stir the dry mixture and break up any lumps.

The wet mixture is always stirred with a fork.

The wet and dry mixtures must be kept separate until just before baking, as liquid activates the raising agent.

When the oven has reached the correct temperature, you are ready to mix the batter. At this point, be sure to do a last minute check to see that you have added all the ingredients.

Using a flexible spatula, scrape all of the wet mixture into the dry, and then use an ordinary metal dessert spoon to combine the ingredients lightly. A metal spoon is more effective than a wooden one for scraping the bottom and sides of the bowl as you bring

the wet and dry together. When you see that all the flour has been moistened and the mixture looks uniform (with small lumps), stop mixing and spoon the batter into the muffin cups.

Most muffin batters should be neither too thick nor too thin. If the baked muffins are small and dense, it could mean the batter was too dry. If they spread out flat instead of rising to a rounded peak, or sink after baking, the batter was probably too wet. As flours can vary in their capacity to absorb liquid, a small adjustment might be needed in order to get the right batter consistency. Please read the important information about flour on pages 12 and 128.

1 Sift the flour, raising agent, and salt together for even distribution.

2 Beat the egg with a fork until frothy, about 10 seconds. Stir in the sugar.

3 Continue to add the other ingredients as specified. Keep the wet and dry mixtures separate until the oven has reached the correct temperature—about 15 minutes for a large oven.

4 Pour all of the wet mixture into the dry mixture. Scrape with a flexible spatula to retain all the liquid.

5 With a metal spoon, combine the wet and dry mixtures using light strokes, with the aim of moistening all the flour in about 20–30 seconds. Avoid stirring round and round. Instead mix efficiently, scraping the bottom and sides of the bowl with the spoon to bring in any dry flour. Use just enough strokes to bring it all together. The batter should appear lumpy but evenly mixed.

6 Immediately spoon the batter into the muffin cups and bake in a preheated, moderately hot oven.

BAKING

Muffins should be baked in a preheated oven at a moderately hot temperature of 190°C (375°F). An oven temperature that is too high or low will impede the rising. Standard-size muffins should start to rise within five minutes of baking, and be well risen and lightly browned in 20–22 minutes. If you find the muffins are fully baked in less than 20 minutes or more than 23, you should adjust your oven temperature accordingly for future batches.

After 20 minutes of baking, open the oven door and touch one of the tops lightly with your finger. If your finger leaves an indent or the muffins look pale, continue baking another 2 minutes and check again. Muffins are done when they hold their shape and have a good colour. Some tops feel firm when baked while others feel a bit springy. The important thing is that they should keep their shape after the touch test. Avoid over-baking as this will dry out the muffins.

Several factors can prevent good rising, such as inadequate preheating, wrong oven temperature, stale or incorrect raising agents, and poor wet/dry balance.

COOLING AND STORING

Muffins will come out of the paper cases or greased pan more easily if you allow them to cool for several minutes after baking.

If a muffin is sticking to its paper case, you can slip a knife just inside the case and run it around the muffin to release it.

Due to the low sugar and fat content of these recipes, they are best served on the day of baking. Ideally, any leftover muffins should be frozen on the same day in airtight bags to maintain freshness. If freezing is not possible, store them in an airtight container and eat within two days. Re-heat to restore freshness.

To thaw a frozen muffin quickly, you can microwave it for 30–40 seconds at Medium. With a regular oven, wrap the frozen muffins loosely in foil and place in a hot oven for about 15 minutes.

KNOW YOUR INGREDIENTS

Each recipe in this book has been carefully crafted to ensure optimum rising, flavour, and texture. If you change the chemistry of the batter, you could end up with something quite different! Having said that, muffins are remarkably adaptable if you understand your ingredients.

FLOUR varies according to the type of wheat it is milled from, whether hard or soft wheat. But to understand flour, we first need to understand gluten. Gluten is formed when the proteins in flour become wet and start linking together. With stirring, these strands become longer and increasingly elastic. Most types of bread need good gluten development to create a springy texture. To achieve this, a high-protein flour (from hard wheat) is used and the dough is well-worked. For most other baked goods, just a small amount of gluten is desired, to give a nice bit of chewy texture. This is normally achieved by using a low-protein flour (from soft wheat) and adding large amounts of sugar and/or fat to inhibit gluten development even when the batter is beaten, as with cake batters.

Since muffins are proportionately lower in sugar and fat than cake, a different strategy is needed for in-hibiting gluten development. The solution is the light mixing tech-nique which reduces the formation of gluten strands and prevents them from becoming elastic. Light mixing is essential for producing a light texture in muffins.

If you are using flour that is not British plain cake flour, please refer to the guidelines on page 128 as the recipes might need to be adjusted. Flour that is used for bread-making (that is, hard wheat flour) is more absorbent than soft wheat flour and requires a little extra liquid.

For those who enjoy wholemeal flour, I would recommend a half-and-half combination to maintain a light texture. Even substituting a small amount of wholemeal flour, such as 50g, will increase fibre and nutritional content.

For gluten- and wheat-free baking, please see page 127.

BAKING POWDER AND BICARBONATE OF SODA are not interchangeable! Baking powder contains both acid and alkaline substances which react together to form tiny bubbles when liquid is added. These bubbles expand when heated, causing the batter to rise. Bicarbonate of soda is simply alkaline, and therefore is not a substitute for baking powder.

After extensive testing, I found myself questioning the common practice of using bicarbonate of soda in combination with certain acidic ingredients. To avoid unpleasant effects in flavour and colour, please be careful to use the raising agents exactly as specified in each recipe.

However, one exception to this would be high altitude baking. The recipes in this book have been tested at sea level. If you live 5,000 feet (1.5 km) or more above sea level, you should reduce the amount of baking powder by about half.

SALT plays a vital role in the chemistry and flavour of baking. The small amount of salt in these recipes should not be omitted! I have fond childhood memories of my mother taking delicious baking out of the oven week by week but, on rare occasions, would hear her groan: 'Oh no, I forgot the salt!' Omission of salt in baking produces sub-standard results—flat flavour along with poor texture and appearance. In addition, the loss of flavour often prompts the addition of extra sugar to compensate. If you need to reduce salt in your diet, it is better to cut back on processed foods rather than eliminate salt from your baking.

EGG enhances the texture and nutritional value of baked goods. The egg should be beaten with a fork until frothy, about 10 seconds, to ensure even distribution in the batter. You don't want to find a lump of cooked egg in your muffin! If you need to omit the egg, add an extra 2 tablespoons of milk.

SUGAR is needed for both flavour and texture. Where a range is given, I would recommend starting mid-range until you find your preferred level of sweetness. For sugar-restricted diets, it can be reduced as low as 1–2 tablespoons but should not be omitted. Note that sugar is added to the wet ingredients to improve absorption in the batter. If you are measuring by volume, please see page 128 for cup conversions.

FAT is essential for good texture in baking. Cooking oil produces a light non-greasy texture in muffins. Choose a mild oil such as vegetable, rapeseed, corn, or sunflower oil. Butter is used in some recipes to add a buttery flavour and additional moistness.

MILK contributes to the nutrition, flavour, and texture of baked goods. For a dairy-free diet, alternative products such as soya milk can be substituted. It might be worth mentioning that whole-milk yogurt is not a high-fat food, and has nutritional and culinary benefits over low fat alternatives.

BUTTERMILK is a naturally low fat product with a pleasant tangy flavour. If buttermilk is unavail-able, you can make a substitute by combining natural yogurt and milk in equal parts. (Do not omit milk specified elsewhere in the recipe.)

FRESH FRUIT AND VEGETABLES release liquid into the batter during baking, whereas dried fruit absorbs liquid. This should be kept in mind when adapting recipes, as the liquid might need to be adjusted by 1–2 tablespoons.

LEMON JUICE is commonly used for souring milk, supposedly to produce a lighter product. In my experience, the opposite is true. It causes the milk to curdle rather than sour, which means the milk has separated into curds and whey, and the final result is a heavier product. Lemon juice should be added at the final mixing to give a boost of acidity without curdling the milk. (Be sure to keep it nearby so you don't forget it!)

ZEST is the thin outer layer of a lemon or orange. It needs to be finely grated to release the flavourful oils; a zester or peeler is not sufficient. Rub the fruit over a rough grater using a circular motion. Continue this, one section at a time, until the yellow (or orange) layer has been removed. Avoid grating into the white pith which is bitter.

UNSWEETENED COCOA POWDER AND DARK CHOCOLATE both contribute dietary minerals including iron and magnesium. Note that cocoa powder mixes best in fat and therefore should be added to the wet ingredients. When choosing chocolate chips for baking, try to select dark chocolate with a minimum of 50% cocoa solids. Dark chocolate will contribute more flavour in baking than milk chocolate, and with less sugar.

WHEAT BRAN is a rich source of beneficial dietary fibre and nutrients. It can be found in health food shops and some supermarkets. Please note that oat bran differs significantly from wheat bran, and is not a suitable substitute in these recipes.

Chocolate

Chocolate

Chocolate Apricot

Chocolate Beetroot

Chocolate Cheesecake

Chocolate Chip

Chocolate Orange

Chocolate Pear

Chocolate Raspberry

Chocolate Ripple

Cocoa Courgette

Mocha Cheesecake

Mocha Cherry

Chocolate Muffins

250g plain white flour (see page 128)

1½ teaspoons baking powder

½ teaspoon bicarbonate of soda

¼ teaspoon salt

4–5 tablespoons dark chocolate chips

1 egg, medium or large

85–100g white granulated sugar (⅓–½ c)

100ml vegetable oil

40g (6 tablespoons) cocoa powder

250ml milk

50ml water

25g butter, melted (2 tablespoons)

Optional topping: chopped or grated
dark chocolate

1 Preheat the oven to 190°C (375°F), Gas Mark 5, fan oven 170°C. Prepare the muffin pan.

2 In a large bowl, sift together flour, baking powder, bicarbonate of soda, and salt. Add chocolate chips.

3 In a medium-sized bowl, beat egg briskly with a fork. Stir well after each addition: sugar, oil, cocoa, milk, water, and butter.

4 When the oven is ready, pour all of wet mixture into dry. With a metal spoon, mix lightly just until combined and no dry flour is visible, about 20–30 seconds. With cocoa batter, a few extra strokes are often needed for moistening the flour, but do not beat or over stir. This batter is thinner than most.

5 Spoon into 12 standard muffin cups. Sprinkle with chocolate. Bake about 20–22 minutes until done. Do not overbake.

Chocolate Iced Muffins Omit chocolate chips and topping. Combine 1 tablespoon melted butter and 1 tablespoon cocoa powder. Add 1 tablespoon warm water and 100g sifted icing sugar (¾ c). Stir until smooth. Add a few drops of water to thin as needed. Spread thinly on muffin tops.

A double chocolate treat

Apricots
are rich in
nutrients

Chocolate Apricot Muffins

250g plain white flour (see page 128)

1½ teaspoons baking powder

½ teaspoon bicarbonate of soda

¼ teaspoon salt

3–4 tablespoons dark chocolate chips (optional)

1 egg, medium or large

85–100g white granulated sugar (⅓–½ c)

100ml vegetable oil

40g (6 tablespoons) cocoa powder

150ml milk

1 tablespoon water

75g dried apricots (about 12), diced

200g fresh or tinned pitted apricots (about 1¼ c sliced)—for purée

100ml water—for purée

1 Preheat the oven to 190°C (375°F), Gas Mark 5, fan oven 170°C. Prepare the muffin pan.

2 Prepare purée at least 30 minutes in advance to allow for cooling. Slice the fresh/tinned apricots and put into a small saucepan with 100ml water. (Do not peel fresh apricots.) Bring to the boil, reduce heat, cover, and simmer 5 minutes. Do not drain. Mash thoroughly to make a wet lumpy purée, and cool completely. (If the purée is too warm, the raising agents will over-react during mixing.) This makes about 250ml purée. Dice the dried apricots and set aside.

3 In a large bowl, sift together flour, baking powder, bicarbonate of soda, and salt. Add chocolate if using.

4 In a medium-sized bowl, beat egg briskly with a fork. Stir well after each addition: sugar, oil, cocoa, milk, 1 tablespoon water, dried apricots, and cooled purée.

5 When the oven is ready, pour all of wet mixture into dry. With a metal spoon, mix lightly just until combined and no dry flour is visible, about 20–30 seconds.

6 Spoon into cups. Bake about 20–22 minutes. Makes 12.

Chocolate Beetroot Muffins

250g plain white flour (see page 128)

1½ teaspoons baking powder

½ teaspoon bicarbonate of soda

¼ teaspoon salt

3–4 tablespoons dark chocolate chips

1 egg, medium or large

85–100g white granulated sugar (⅓–½ c)

100ml vegetable oil

40g (6 tablespoons) cocoa powder

200ml buttermilk*

100ml milk

150ml puréed cooked beetroot
(ready-cooked beetroot is available
in some supermarkets)

*Buttermilk alternative: 100ml yogurt
plus 100ml (extra) milk*

1   Boil 2–3 whole small beetroot (minimum 300g total) about
40 minutes until tender. Drain, peel, and purée. Measure 150ml.

2   Preheat the oven to 190°C (375°F), Gas Mark 5, fan oven 170°C.
Prepare the muffin pan.

3   In a large bowl, sift together flour, baking powder, bicarbonate
of soda, and salt. Add chocolate chips.

4   In a medium-sized bowl, beat egg briskly with a fork. Stir well
after each addition: sugar, oil, cocoa, buttermilk, milk, and
beetroot purée.

5   When the oven is ready, pour wet mixture into dry. Mix lightly
with a metal spoon just until combined and no dry flour is
visible, about 20–30 seconds. With cocoa batter, a few extra
strokes are usually needed, but do not beat or over stir.

6   Fill cups nearly full. Bake about 20–22 minutes. Makes 12.

Luscious
but not
decadent

Chocolate Cheesecake Muffins

250g plain white flour (see page 128)

1½ teaspoons baking powder

½ teaspoon bicarbonate of soda

¼ teaspoon salt

1 egg, medium or large

85–100g white granulated sugar (⅓–½ c)

100ml vegetable oil

40g (6 tablespoons) cocoa powder

300ml milk

1 tablespoon water

Filling:

150g full fat cream cheese

2 tablespoons white granulated sugar

20g dark chocolate, coarsely grated
   (4 tablespoons)

Optional topping: grated chocolate

1   Preheat the oven to 190°C (375°F), Gas Mark 5, fan oven 170°C. Prepare the muffin pan.

2   Stir filling ingredients together and set aside. Prepare 2 tablespoons grated chocolate for topping if using.

3   In a large bowl, sift together flour, baking powder, bicarbonate of soda, and salt.

4   In a medium-sized bowl, beat egg briskly with a fork. Stir well after each addition: sugar, oil, cocoa, milk, and water.

5   When the oven is ready, pour wet mixture into dry. With a metal spoon, mix lightly just until combined and no dry flour is visible, about 20–30 seconds. With cocoa batter, a few extra strokes are often needed, but do not beat or over stir.

6   Put a spoonful of batter into each muffin cup to cover the base. Add a generous teaspoon of filling to each, and then top with remaining batter. Sprinkle with grated chocolate. Bake about 20–22 minutes until done. Makes 12.

Photo: page 16, top

Chocolate Chip Muffins

275g plain white flour (see page 128)

2¼ teaspoons baking powder

¼ teaspoon salt

4–6 tablespoons dark or milk chocolate chips

1 egg, medium or large

75–100g white granulated sugar (⅓–½ c)

100ml vegetable oil

200ml milk

60g finely chopped red apple (⅓ c); *or* 50ml yogurt; *or* 1 tablespoon milk

25g butter, melted (2 tablespoons)

1. Preheat the oven to 190°C (375°F), Gas Mark 5, fan oven 170°C. Prepare the muffin pan.

2. In a large bowl, sift together flour, baking powder, and salt. Add chocolate chips.

3. In a medium-sized bowl, beat egg briskly with a fork. Stir well after each addition: sugar, oil, milk, apple, and butter.

4. When the oven is ready, pour wet mixture into dry. Using a metal spoon, mix lightly just until combined and no dry flour is visible, about 20 seconds. Do not beat or over stir.

5. Spoon batter into cups. Sprinkle with extra chocolate chips if desired. Bake about 20–22 minutes until lightly browned. Makes 12.

Mandarins add a fruity sweetness

Chocolate Orange Muffins

250g plain white flour (see page 128)

1¼ teaspoons baking powder

½ teaspoon bicarbonate of soda

¼ teaspoon salt

3–4 tablespoons dark chocolate chips

1 egg, medium or large

85–100g white granulated sugar (⅓–½ c)

100ml vegetable oil

40g (6 tablespoons) cocoa powder

2 teaspoons finely grated orange zest
(of 2 firm juice oranges)

150ml milk

50ml water

50ml fresh orange juice

175g tinned mandarin orange segments,*
drained and sliced in thirds (1 c)

*Tinned mandarin segments are sweeter
and less fibrous than fresh.*

1   Preheat the oven to 190°C (375°F), Gas Mark 5, fan oven 170°C. Prepare the muffin pan.

2   In a large bowl, sift together flour, baking powder, bicarbonate of soda, and salt. Add chocolate chips.

3   In a medium-sized bowl, beat egg briskly with a fork. Stir well after each addition: sugar, oil, cocoa, zest, milk, water, and juice. Prepare mandarin segments but do not add them yet.

4   When the oven is ready, pour all of wet mixture into dry. With a metal spoon, mix lightly just until combined and no dry flour is visible, about 20–30 seconds. Gently fold in mandarin pieces. Do not over stir.

5   Fill cups nearly full. Bake about 20–22 minutes until done. Makes 12.

Chocolate Pear Muffins

250g plain white flour (see page 128)

1½ teaspoons baking powder

½ teaspoon bicarbonate of soda

¼ teaspoon salt

1 egg, medium or large

75–100g white granulated sugar (⅓–½ c)

100ml vegetable oil

40g (6 tablespoons) cocoa powder

150ml milk

100ml tinned pear juice*

200g tinned pears, chopped (1 c)

*With fresh pears, use milk instead of juice.

1 Preheat the oven to 190°C (375°F), Gas Mark 5, fan oven 170°C. Prepare the muffin pan.

2 In a large bowl, sift together flour, baking powder, bicarbonate of soda, and salt.

3 In a medium-sized bowl, beat egg briskly with a fork. Stir well after each addition: sugar, oil, cocoa, milk, juice, and chopped pears.

4 When the oven is ready, pour all of wet mixture into dry. With a metal spoon, mix lightly just until combined and no dry flour is visible, about 20–30 seconds.

5 Fill cups nearly full. Bake about 20–22 minutes until done. Makes 12.

Use tinned pears to enjoy these year round

A delicious blend of sweet and tart

Chocolate Raspberry Muffins

250g plain white flour (see page 128)

1 teaspoon baking powder

½ teaspoon bicarbonate of soda

¼ teaspoon salt

3–4 tablespoons dark chocolate chips

1 egg, medium or large

85–100g white granulated sugar (⅓–½ c)

100ml vegetable oil

40g (6 tablespoons) cocoa powder

100ml sour cream (cultured)

200ml milk

150g raspberries, quartered (1 c); do not thaw if frozen

Optional toppings: 4 raspberries, finely chopped; 10g dark chocolate, grated (2 tablespoons)

1   Preheat the oven to 190°C (375°F), Gas Mark 5, fan oven 170°C. Prepare the muffin pan.

2   In a large bowl, sift together flour, baking powder, bicarbonate of soda, and salt. Add chocolate chips.

3   In a medium-sized bowl, beat egg briskly with a fork. Stir well after each addition: sugar, oil, cocoa, sour cream, and milk. Prepare berries but do not add them to the batter.

4   When the oven is ready, pour wet mixture into dry. With a metal spoon, mix lightly just until combined and no dry flour is visible, about 20–30 seconds.

5   Put a spoonful of batter into each cup to cover the base. Distribute half the berries. Gently fold the remaining berries into the batter in the bowl. Spoon out this batter and sprinkle sparingly with berry seeds. Bake about 20–22 minutes until done. Frozen fruit might require an extra 2–3 minutes. Sprinkle hot tops with grated chocolate if desired. Makes 12.

Chocolate Ripple Muffins

275g plain white flour (see page 128)

1½ teaspoons baking powder

¼ teaspoon bicarbonate of soda

¼ teaspoon salt

1 egg, medium or large

75–100g white granulated sugar (⅓–½ c)

100ml vegetable oil

200ml buttermilk*

100ml milk

Filling:

25g (2 tablespoons) butter

2 tablespoons light brown soft sugar

½ teaspoon ground cinnamon

75g dark chocolate, coarsely chopped

4 teaspoons water

Topping: grated chocolate and pecans

*Or 100ml yogurt plus 100ml (extra) milk

1 Preheat the oven to 190°C (375°F), Gas Mark 5, fan oven 170°C. Prepare the muffin pan.

2 Place filling ingredients in a heatproof bowl over (but not in) a pot of simmering water. Stir just until melted and then set aside to cool. (High heat can spoil the texture of chocolate.) Prepare grated chocolate for topping.

3 In a large bowl, sift together flour, baking powder, bicarbonate of soda, and salt.

4 In a medium-sized bowl, beat egg briskly with a fork. Stir in sugar, oil, buttermilk, and milk.

5 When the oven is ready, pour wet mixture into dry. With a metal spoon, mix lightly just until combined, about 20 seconds. Buttermilk batter is thick. Do not over stir.

6 Drop a spoonful of batter into each cup to cover the base. If the chocolate filling has thickened, add an extra teaspoon of water. Drizzle a generous teaspoon of filling into each cup. Top with remaining batter, grated chocolate, and a pecan. Bake about 20–22 minutes until lightly browned. Makes 12.

Deliciously sophisticated

Cocoa Courgette Muffins

250g plain white flour (see page 128)

1½ teaspoons baking powder

½ teaspoon bicarbonate of soda

¼ teaspoon salt

2 teaspoons ground cinnamon

1 egg, medium or large

2 tablespoons light brown soft sugar

50–75g white granulated sugar (¼–⅓ c)

125ml vegetable oil

40g (6 tablespoons) cocoa powder

300g finely grated courgette (1¼ c)

100ml milk

2 tablespoons water

75g raisins or sultanas (½ c)

1   Preheat the oven to 190°C (375°F), Gas Mark 5, fan oven 170°C. Prepare the muffin pan.

2   Peel the courgette (also known as zucchini) and grate finely. As the courgette provides most of the liquid, chopping is not adequate.

3   In a large bowl, sift together flour, baking powder, bicarbonate of soda, salt, and cinnamon.

4   In a medium-sized bowl, beat egg briskly with a fork. Stir well after each addition: brown and white sugar, oil, cocoa, courgette, milk, water, and raisins.

5   When the oven is ready, pour wet mixture into dry. With a metal spoon, mix lightly just until combined and no dry flour is visible, about 20–30 seconds. Do not beat or over stir.

6   Fill cups nearly full. Bake about 20–22 minutes until done. Makes 12.

Photo: page 16, bottom

Mocha Cheesecake Muffins

250g plain white flour (see page 128)

1½ teaspoons baking powder

½ teaspoon bicarbonate of soda

¼ teaspoon salt

1 egg, medium or large

75–100g white granulated sugar (⅓–½ c)

100ml vegetable oil

25g (4 tablespoons) cocoa powder

150ml milk

3 tablespoons instant coffee granules
  dissolved in 150ml boiling water

Filling:

150g full fat cream cheese

2 tablespoons white granulated sugar

20g dark chocolate, coarsely grated
  (4 tablespoons)

Optional topping: grated chocolate

1 Preheat the oven to 190°C (375°F), Gas Mark 5, fan oven 170°C. Prepare the muffin pan.

2 Dissolve coffee granules in 150ml boiling water and set aside to cool. Stir filling ingredients together and set aside. Prepare 2 tablespoons grated chocolate for topping.

3 In a large bowl, sift together flour, baking powder, bicarbonate of soda, and salt.

4 In another bowl, beat egg briskly with a fork. Stir well after each addition: sugar, oil, cocoa, milk, and cooled coffee.

5 When the oven is ready, pour wet into dry. With a metal spoon, mix lightly just until combined and no dry flour is visible, about 20–30 seconds. This batter is thinner than most.

6 Put a spoonful of batter into each muffin cup to cover the base. Add a heaped teaspoon of filling to each, and top with remaining batter. Bake about 20–22 minutes until done. Immediately after baking, sprinkle hot tops with grated chocolate if desired. Makes 12.

A classic
combination

Mocha Cherry Muffins

250g plain white flour (see page 128)

1 teaspoon baking powder

½ teaspoon bicarbonate of soda

¼ teaspoon salt

1 egg, medium or large

85–100g white granulated sugar (⅓–½ c)

100ml vegetable oil

40g (6 tablespoons) cocoa powder

100ml sour cream (cultured)

50ml milk

3 tablespoons instant coffee granules
    dissolved in 150ml boiling water

200g pitted cherries, fresh or tinned (1¼ c)

Optional Chocolate Sauce:

2½ teaspoons cornflour (cornstarch)

250ml milk

4 tablespoons white granulated sugar

4 tablespoons cocoa powder

2 tablespoons butter

1   Preheat the oven to 190°C (375°F), Gas Mark 5, fan oven 170°C. Prepare the muffin pan.

2   Dissolve coffee granules in 150ml boiling water and set aside to cool. Prepare cherries by cutting into quarters.

3   In a large bowl, sift together flour, baking powder, bicarbonate of soda, and salt.

4   In a separate bowl, beat egg briskly with a fork. Stir well after each addition: sugar, oil, cocoa, sour cream, milk, and coffee mixture.

5   When the oven is ready, pour wet mixture into dry. With a metal spoon, mix lightly just until combined and no dry flour is visible, about 20–30 seconds.

6   Put a spoonful of batter into each cup to cover the base. Distribute cherries evenly, and top with remaining batter. Bake about 20–22 minutes. Makes 12.

7   For the chocolate sauce, stir cornflour and cold milk together in a small saucepan until smooth. Add sugar, cocoa, and butter. Place over low heat and stir constantly until smooth and bubbling, about 2 minutes. Remove from heat; do not overheat. Makes 2 tablespoons sauce per muffin.

Nuts and
Oats

Apricot Almond
Butter Pecan
Cinnamon Swirl
Coffee Date
Cranberry Oat
Fruit 'n' Spice
Granola
Hazelnut and Chocolate
Maple
Oat Chocolate Chip
Oat Pear
Peanut Butter

Apricot Almond Muffins

275g plain white flour (see page 128)

2¼ teaspoons baking powder

¼ teaspoon salt

1 egg, medium or large

75–100g white granulated sugar (⅓–½ c)

100ml vegetable oil

50ml natural yogurt

200ml milk

25g butter, melted (2 tablespoons)

175g dried apricots (1 c)

Topping: flaked almonds

1 Preheat the oven to 190°C (375°F), Gas Mark 5, fan oven 170°C. Prepare the muffin pan.

2 Pour boiling water over dried apricots in a bowl, and let soak about 10 minutes. Drain and dice.

3 In a large bowl, sift together flour, baking powder, and salt.

4 In a medium-sized bowl, beat egg briskly with a fork. Stir in sugar, oil, yogurt, milk, butter, and chopped apricots.

5 When the oven is ready, pour wet mixture into dry. Mix lightly with a metal spoon just until combined and no dry flour is visible, about 20 seconds. Do not over stir.

6 Fill cups nearly full. Sprinkle generously with almonds. Bake about 20–22 minutes until lightly browned. Makes 12.

A winning combination of flavours

Inspired by the classic Canadian butter tart

Butter Pecan Muffins

250g plain white flour (see page 128)

1½ teaspoons baking powder

½ teaspoon bicarbonate of soda

¼ teaspoon salt

1 egg, medium or large

75–100g light brown soft sugar (⅓–½ c)

250ml milk

1 tablespoon water

75g currants or raisins (½ c)*

75g pecans, chopped (⅔ c)

100g butter, melted (½ c)

Topping:

1 tablespoon butter, melted

1–2 tablespoons light brown soft sugar

40g pecans, chopped (⅓ c)

*If your dried fruit has become too dry,
leave it to soak in boiling hot water for
5 minutes, then drain.*

1   Preheat the oven to 190°C (375°F), Gas Mark 5, fan oven 170°C. Prepare the muffin pan.

2   Combine topping ingredients and set aside.

3   In a large bowl, sift together flour, baking powder, bicarbonate of soda, and salt.

4   In a medium-sized bowl, beat egg briskly with a fork. Add sugar, milk, water, currants, pecans, and butter.

5   When the oven is ready, pour wet mixture into dry. With a metal spoon, mix lightly just until combined and no dry flour is visible, about 20 seconds. Do not over stir. This batter is wetter than most.

6   Fill cups nearly full. Distribute topping. Bake about 20–22 minutes until lightly browned. Makes 12.

Cinnamon Swirl Muffins

250g plain white flour (see page 128)

1½ teaspoons baking powder

¼ teaspoon bicarbonate of soda

¼ teaspoon salt

1 egg, medium or large

75–100g white granulated sugar (⅓–½ c)

100ml vegetable oil

150ml milk

150ml sour cream (cultured)

2 tablespoons water

Filling and Topping:

2 tablespoons light brown soft sugar

2 teaspoons ground cinnamon

100g pecans or walnuts, chopped (¾ c)

1   Preheat the oven to 190°C (375°F), Gas Mark 5, fan oven 170°C. Prepare the muffin pan.

2   Prepare the filling and topping mixture, and set aside. (Nuts can be omitted if preferred.)

3   In a large bowl, sift together flour, baking powder, bicarbonate of soda, and salt.

4   In a medium-sized bowl, beat egg briskly with a fork. Stir in white sugar, oil, milk, sour cream, and water.

5   When the oven is ready, pour wet mixture into dry. With a metal spoon, mix lightly just until combined and no dry flour is visible, about 20 seconds. Do not beat or over stir.

6   Put a spoonful of batter into each muffin cup to cover the base. Distribute half the cinnamon mixture. Spoon out the remaining batter and finish with the other half of the cinnamon mixture. Bake about 20–22 minutes until lightly browned. Makes 12.

An enticing
sour cream
muffin

Coffee Date Muffins

275g plain white flour (see page 128)

1½ teaspoons baking powder

½ teaspoon bicarbonate of soda

¼ teaspoon salt

1 egg, medium or large

75–100g light brown soft sugar (⅓–½ c)

150ml milk

3 tablespoons instant coffee granules
dissolved in 150ml boiling water

150g dried dates, chopped (1 c)

100g butter, melted (½ c)

Optional topping: 12 walnut halves

1 Preheat the oven to 190°C (375°F), Gas Mark 5, fan oven 170°C. Prepare the muffin pan.

2 Dissolve coffee granules in 150ml boiling water. Pour over chopped dates in a bowl, and leave this to soak and cool for 10 minutes. Do not drain.

3 In a large bowl, sift together flour, baking powder, bicarbonate of soda, and salt.

4 In a medium-sized bowl, beat egg briskly with a fork. Stir in sugar, milk, cooled coffee/dates, and melted butter.

5 When the oven is ready, pour wet mixture into dry. Mix lightly with a metal spoon just until combined and no dry flour is visible, about 20 seconds. Do not over stir.

6 Fill cups nearly full. Top with walnut halves if using. Bake about 20–22 minutes until done. Makes 12.

Photo: page 38, left

Cranberry Oat Muffins

250g plain white flour (see page 128)

1½ teaspoons baking powder

¼ teaspoon bicarbonate of soda

¼ teaspoon salt

1 egg, medium or large

75–100g white granulated sugar (⅓–½ c)

100ml vegetable oil

150ml natural yogurt

200ml milk

50g rolled oats (½ c)

100g cranberries, chopped (1 c)

1   Preheat the oven to 190°C (375°F), Gas Mark 5, fan oven 170°C. Prepare the muffin pan.

2   In a large bowl, sift together flour, baking powder, bicarbonate of soda, and salt.

3   In a medium-sized bowl, beat egg briskly with a fork. Stir in sugar, oil, yogurt, milk, oats, and cranberries.

4   When the oven is ready, pour wet mixture into dry. With a metal spoon, mix lightly just until combined and no dry flour is visible, about 20 seconds. Do not beat or over stir.

5   Spoon into muffin cups. Sprinkle tops with a pinch of sugar if desired. Bake about 20–22 minutes until lightly browned. Makes 12.

Sultana Oat Muffins Replace fresh berries with 75g (½ c) dried fruit such as sultanas, raisins, or dried cranberries. Add 1 tablespoon water.

Subtle spices,
warm aromas

Fruit 'n' Spice Muffins

225g plain white flour (see page 128)

1½ teaspoons baking powder

½ teaspoon bicarbonate of soda

¼ teaspoon salt

1 teaspoon ground cinnamon

½ teaspoon ground cloves

¼ teaspoon ground nutmeg

1 egg, medium or large

75–100g light brown soft sugar (⅓–½ c)

100ml vegetable oil

250ml milk

100g finely chopped sweet red apple (⅔ c)

50g raisins (⅓ c)

50g dried dates, chopped (⅓ c)

50g rolled oats (½ c)

Optional topping: brown sugar

1   Preheat the oven to 190°C (375°F), Gas Mark 5, fan oven 170°C. Prepare the muffin pan.

2   Pour boiling water over dates and let soak for 5 minutes. Drain and chop. Chop apple and set aside.

3   In a large bowl, sift together flour, baking powder, bicarbonate of soda, salt, and spices.

4   In a medium-sized bowl, beat egg briskly with a fork. Stir in sugar, oil, milk, apple, raisins, dates, and oats.

5   When the oven is ready, pour wet mixture into dry. With a metal spoon, mix lightly just until combined and no dry flour is visible, about 20 seconds. Do not beat or over stir.

6   Fill cups nearly full. Sprinkle each top lightly with brown sugar if desired. Bake about 20–22 minutes until lightly browned. Makes 12.

Granola Muffins

250g plain white flour (see page 128)

1½ teaspoons baking powder

¼ teaspoon bicarbonate of soda

¼ teaspoon salt

1 teaspoon cinnamon (optional)

3–4 tablespoons chocolate chips (optional)

1 egg, medium or large

75–100g white granulated sugar (⅓–½ c)

100ml vegetable oil

250ml milk

100ml natural yogurt

Granola Mix,* cooled

Topping: extra seeds or chopped nuts

See opposite page for Granola Mix.

1 Prepare the granola in advance. Preheat the oven to a lower temperature for the granola: 160°C (325°F), Gas Mark 3, fan oven 140°C. Chop almonds and pecans, and combine with oats and seeds. Stir melted butter and maple syrup together and add to oat mixture, stirring well to coat. Spread mixture on a baking sheet, keeping it away from the edges of the pan and about 1cm deep to avoid scorching. Bake about 15 minutes until lightly golden, stirring every 5 minutes. Set aside to cool.

2 Now preheat the oven to 190°C (375°F), Gas Mark 5, fan oven 170°C. Prepare the muffin pan.

3 In a large bowl, sift together flour, baking powder, bicarbonate of soda, salt, and cinnamon. Add chocolate if using.

4 In a medium-sized bowl, beat egg briskly with a fork. Add sugar, oil, milk, and yogurt.

5 When the oven is ready, pour wet mixture into dry, along with Granola Mix. With a metal spoon, mix lightly just until combined and no dry flour is visible, about 20 seconds. Do not over stir.

6 Spoon into cups. Sprinkle with topping. Bake about 20–22 minutes until lightly browned. Makes 12.

Granola Mix:

50g almonds, chopped (⅓ c)

50g pecans, chopped (⅓ c)

50g rolled oats (½ c)

3 tablespoons sunflower seeds

2 tablespoons butter, melted

1 tablespoon pure maple syrup or honey

Chock-full of wholesome goodness

Savour the depth of
roasted hazelnut

Hazelnut and Chocolate Muffins

275g plain white flour (see page 128)

1½ teaspoons baking powder

¼ teaspoon bicarbonate of soda

¼ teaspoon salt

75g dark or milk chocolate, chopped (⅓ c)

75g whole hazelnuts (½ c)

1 egg, medium or large

75–100g white granulated sugar (⅓–½ c)

100ml vegetable oil

200ml buttermilk*

100ml milk

Optional topping: 2 tablespoons grated chocolate

*Buttermilk alternative: 100ml yogurt plus 100ml (extra) milk

1   Preheat the oven to 190°C (375°F), Gas Mark 5, fan oven 170°C. Prepare the muffin pan.

2   Spread whole hazelnuts on a baking sheet, and roast in a preheated oven for 5 minutes to bring out the flavour. Chop nuts and chocolate, and set aside. Prepare topping.

3   In a large bowl, sift together flour, baking powder, bicarbonate of soda, and salt. Add chopped chocolate and nuts.

4   In a medium-sized bowl, beat egg briskly with a fork. Add sugar, oil, buttermilk, and milk.

5   When the oven is ready, pour wet mixture into dry. With a metal spoon, mix lightly just until combined and no dry flour is visible, about 20 seconds. Do not over stir. Buttermilk batter is thick.

6   Fill cups nearly full. Sprinkle with grated chocolate. Bake about 20–22 minutes until lightly browned. Makes 12.

Maple Muffins

225g plain white flour (see page 128)

2½ teaspoons baking powder

¼ teaspoon salt

100g butter (½ c)

1 egg, medium or large

200ml milk

1 tablespoon water

50g rolled oats (½ c)

100ml pure maple syrup

2 tablespoons white granulated sugar

Optional: 50g pecans or walnuts, chopped (⅓ c)

Maple Syrup Glaze:

1 tablespoon soft butter

1 tablespoon maple syrup

60g sifted icing sugar (½ c)

1   Preheat the oven to 190°C (375°F), Gas Mark 5, fan oven 170°C. Prepare the muffin pan.

2   First prepare the nuts if using. Then, in a large bowl, sift together flour, baking powder, and salt. Cut butter into the flour mixture with a pastry blender (or rub together with fingers) until evenly distributed, like fine crumbs.

3   In a medium-sized bowl, beat egg briskly with a fork. Stir in milk, water, oats, maple syrup, and sugar.

4   When the oven is ready, pour wet mixture into dry. Add nuts if using. With a metal spoon, mix lightly just until combined, about 20 seconds. Do not beat or over stir.

5   Fill cups nearly full. Bake about 20–22 minutes until golden brown. Stir glaze ingredients together until smooth, and spread thinly over the hot muffin tops. Makes 12.

A special treat

So simple, so good

Oat Chocolate Chip Muffins

250g plain white flour (see page 128)

2 teaspoons baking powder

¼ teaspoon bicarbonate of soda

¼ teaspoon salt

4–6 tablespoons chocolate chips

1 egg, medium or large

75–100g light brown soft sugar (⅓–½ c)

100ml vegetable oil

250ml milk

2 tablespoons water

50g rolled oats (½ c)

25g butter, melted (2 tablespoons)

1 Preheat the oven to 190°C (375°F), Gas Mark 5, fan oven 170°C. Prepare the muffin pan.

2 In a large bowl, sift together flour, baking powder, bicarbonate of soda, and salt. Add chocolate chips.

3 In a medium-sized bowl, beat egg briskly with a fork. Stir in sugar, oil, milk, water, oats, and butter.

4 When the oven is ready, pour all of wet mixture into dry. With a metal spoon, mix lightly just until combined and no dry flour is visible, about 20 seconds. Do not over stir.

5 Fill cups nearly full. Bake about 20–22 minutes until lightly browned. Makes 12.

Oat Pear Muffins

250g plain white flour (see page 128)

2 teaspoons baking powder

¼ teaspoon bicarbonate of soda

¼ teaspoon salt

3–4 tablespoons dark chocolate chips (optional)

1 egg, medium or large

75–100g white granulated sugar (⅓–½ c)

100ml vegetable oil

200ml milk

1 tablespoon tinned pear juice or water

200g chopped pear, tinned or fresh (1 c)

50g rolled oats (½ c)

1 Preheat the oven to 190°C (375°F), Gas Mark 5, fan oven 170°C. Prepare the muffin pan.

2 In a large bowl, sift together flour, baking powder, bicarbonate of soda, and salt. Add chocolate chips.

3 In a medium-sized bowl, beat egg briskly with a fork. Stir in sugar, oil, milk, juice, pear, and oats.

4 When the oven is ready, pour wet mixture into dry. Mix lightly with a metal spoon just until combined and no dry flour is visible, about 20 seconds. Do not beat or over stir.

5 Fill cups nearly full. Bake about 20–22 minutes until lightly browned. Makes 12.

Photo: page 38, right

Peanut Butter Muffins

225g plain white flour (see page 128)

2 teaspoons baking powder

¼ teaspoon bicarbonate of soda

¼ teaspoon salt

3–4 tablespoons chocolate chips

1 egg, medium or large

75–100g white granulated sugar (⅓–½ c)

100ml vegetable oil

100g (6 tablespoons) peanut butter

250ml milk

2 tablespoons water

50g rolled oats (½ c)

Optional: 12 dried apricots, chopped

1 Preheat the oven to 190°C (375°F), Gas Mark 5, fan oven 170°C. Prepare the muffin pan.

2 In a large bowl, sift together flour, baking powder, bicarbonate of soda, and salt. Add chocolate chips.

3 In a medium-sized bowl, beat egg briskly with a fork. Stir well after each addition: sugar, oil, peanut butter, milk, water, and oats. (Add dried apricots if using.) Continue stirring with a fork until the peanut butter is well distributed.

4 When the oven is ready, pour wet mixture into dry. Mix lightly with a metal spoon just until combined, about 20 seconds. Do not beat or over stir.

5 Fill cups nearly full. Bake about 20–22 minutes until golden brown. Makes 12.

Fruit

Apple Harvest

Apple Layer

Apple Raspberry

Apple Spice

Banana

Banana Tropical

Blueberry

Blueberry Cheesecake

Butternut Squash (Pumpkin)

Carrot Pineapple

Gingerbread Apple

Lemon

Lemon Cheesecake

Lemon-Filled

Mango

Orange

Orange Apricot

Orange Carrot Spice

Peach

Pear Ginger

Pineapple

Plum Orange

Raspberry Lemon

Raspberry and White Chocolate

Rhubarb Almond

Strawberry Rhubarb

Apple Harvest Muffins

250g plain white flour (see page 128)

2½ teaspoons baking powder

¼ teaspoon salt

100g butter (½ c)

1 egg, medium or large

75–100g white granulated sugar (⅓–½ c)

200g finely chopped sweet red apple
  (1⅓ c)

150ml milk

100g raisins (⅔ c)

Topping: white granulated sugar

1　Preheat the oven to 190°C (375°F), Gas Mark 5, fan oven 170°C. Prepare the muffin pan.

2　In a large bowl, sift together flour, baking powder, and salt. Cut in butter with a pastry blender (or rub together with fingers) until evenly distributed, like fine crumbs.

3　In a medium-sized bowl, beat egg briskly with a fork. Add sugar, apple, milk, and raisins.

4　When the oven is ready, pour wet mixture into dry. This batter is thick, so you will need to cut through the mixture with a metal spoon, lifting and combining as you turn the bowl. Mix only until no flour is visible, about 20 seconds.

5　Spoon into muffin cups. Sprinkle each top with a pinch of sugar. Bake about 20–22 minutes until golden brown. Makes 12.

A buttery muffin loaded with fruit

A tasty apple and cinnamon filling

Apple Layer Muffins

250g plain white flour (see page 128)

2½ teaspoons baking powder

¼ teaspoon salt

4 tablespoons wheat germ*

1 egg, medium or large

75–100g white granulated sugar (⅓–½ c)

100ml vegetable oil

250ml milk

Filling:

150g thinly sliced sweet red apple (1 c)

1½ teaspoons ground cinnamon

1–2 tablespoons white granulated sugar

2 tablespoons butter, melted

Wheat germ is nutritious and adds a pleasant nutty flavour. Flour can be substituted if preferred.

1. Preheat the oven to 190°C (375°F), Gas Mark 5, fan oven 170°C. Prepare the muffin pan.

2. Cut peeled apple into thin slices, and then cut the slices into approximate 1cm lengths. Combine cinnamon with 1–2 tablespoons sugar and mix with the apple. Add butter and set aside.

3. In a large bowl, sift together flour, baking powder, and salt. Add wheat germ.

4. In a medium-sized bowl, beat egg briskly with a fork. Stir in sugar, oil, and milk.

5. When the oven is ready, pour wet mixture into dry. With a metal spoon, mix lightly just until combined and no dry flour is visible, about 20 seconds. Do not beat or over stir. This batter is wetter than most.

6. Put a spoonful of batter into each cup to cover the base. Distribute the filling, and finish with remaining batter. Sprinkle each top with a pinch of sugar. Bake about 20–22 minutes until lightly browned. Makes 12.

Apple Raspberry Muffins

275g plain white flour (see page 128)

2½ teaspoons baking powder

¼ teaspoon salt

1 egg, medium or large

75–100g white granulated sugar (⅓–½ c)

100ml vegetable oil

150ml milk

2 tablespoons water

150g sweet red apple, chopped (1 c)

100g raspberries, quartered (⅔ c);
  do not thaw if frozen

Optional toppings: a pinch of granulated
  sugar, or crumble topping

Crumble Topping:

50g rolled oats (½ c)

2 tablespoons light brown soft sugar

25g (2 tablespoons) butter, melted

1 Preheat the oven to 190°C (375°F), Gas Mark 5, fan oven 170°C. Prepare the muffin pan.

2 Prepare the crumble topping if using. Set aside.

3 In a large bowl, sift together flour, baking powder, and salt.

4 In a medium-sized bowl, beat egg briskly with a fork. Add sugar, oil, milk, water, and apple. Prepare the berries and set aside; do not add them to the batter.

5 When the oven is ready, pour wet mixture into dry. With a metal spoon, mix lightly just until combined, about 20 seconds. Do not over stir. This batter is quite thick.

6 Put a spoonful of batter into each cup to cover the base. Distribute most of the berries. Gently fold the remainder into the batter in the bowl. Spoon out this batter and sprinkle with your choice of topping. Bake about 20–22 minutes until lightly browned. Frozen fruit might require an extra 2–3 minutes. Makes 12.

Apple Blueberry Muffins Replace raspberries with blueberries but do not quarter.

Photo: page 60, top

Apple Spice Muffins

275g plain white flour (see page 128)

2½ teaspoons baking powder

¼ teaspoon salt

2 teaspoons mixed spice*

1 egg, medium or large

75–100g white granulated sugar (⅓–½ c)

100ml vegetable oil

150ml milk

2 tablespoons water or milk

200g finely chopped sweet red apple
  (1⅓ c)

Optional topping:

1 tablespoon light brown soft sugar

50g walnuts, chopped (⅓ c)

**Mixed spice can be replaced with
1½ teaspoons ground cinnamon plus
¼ teaspoon each of ground nutmeg,
cloves, and ginger.*

1   Preheat the oven to 190°C (375°F), Gas Mark 5, fan oven 170°C. Prepare the muffin pan.

2   Combine topping ingredients and set aside. (Note: Nuts can be added to the batter or omitted if preferred.)

3   In a large bowl, sift together flour, baking powder, salt, and spice.

4   In a medium-sized bowl, beat egg briskly with a fork. Stir in sugar, oil, milk, water, and apple.

5   When the oven is ready, pour wet mixture into dry. With a metal spoon, mix lightly just until combined, about 20 seconds. Do not over stir. The batter will be quite thick as apple releases juice during baking.

6   Fill cups nearly full. Sprinkle with topping. Bake about 20–22 minutes until lightly browned. Makes 12.

Banana Muffins

275g plain white flour (see page 128)

1½ teaspoons baking powder

½ teaspoon bicarbonate of soda

¼ teaspoon salt

1 egg, medium or large

75–100g white granulated sugar (⅓–½ c)

100ml vegetable oil

300ml or 300g ripe banana purée (about 3 medium)

100ml milk

2 tablespoons water or milk

Optional: 50g chocolate chips (¼ c) or chopped walnuts (⅓ c)

Tip: Ripe bananas can be frozen in an air-tight container or bag for future use.

1 Preheat the oven to 190°C (375°F), Gas Mark 5, fan oven 170°C. Prepare the muffin pan.

2 Mash bananas thoroughly to make a wet lumpy purée. You can use either a potato masher or an electric blender. Measure 300ml.

3 In a large bowl, sift together flour, baking powder, bicarbonate of soda, and salt. (Add chocolate chips if using.)

4 In a medium-sized bowl, beat egg briskly with a fork. Stir in sugar, oil, banana purée, milk, and water.

5 When the oven is ready, pour wet mixture into dry. (Add nuts if using.) With a metal spoon, mix lightly just until combined and no dry flour is visible, about 20 seconds. Do not beat or over stir.

6 Fill cups nearly full. Bake about 20–22 minutes until lightly browned. Makes 12.

An all-time
favourite

An exotic blend with pineapple and coconut

Banana Tropical Muffins

275g plain white flour (see page 128)

1½ teaspoons baking powder

½ teaspoon bicarbonate of soda

¼ teaspoon salt

1 egg, medium or large

75–100g white granulated sugar (⅓–½ c)

100ml vegetable oil

150ml ripe banana purée (2 medium)

150ml milk

150g pineapple (4 tinned slices),
    chopped (⅔ c)

Optional topping: desiccated coconut

1. Preheat the oven to 190°C (375°F), Gas Mark 5, fan oven 170°C. Prepare the muffin pan.

2. Mash bananas thoroughly to make a wet lumpy purée. You can use either a potato masher or an electric blender. Measure 150ml.

3. In a large bowl, sift together flour, baking powder, bicarbonate of soda, and salt.

4. In a medium-sized bowl, beat egg briskly with a fork. Stir in sugar, oil, banana purée, milk, and pineapple.

5. When the oven is ready, pour wet mixture into dry. Mix lightly with a metal spoon just until combined and no dry flour is visible, about 20 seconds. Do not beat or over stir.

6. Fill cups nearly full. Sprinkle generously with coconut. Bake about 20–22 minutes until golden brown. Makes 12.

Blueberry Muffins

275g plain white flour (see page 128)

2¼ teaspoons baking powder

¼ teaspoon salt

1 egg, medium or large

75–100g white granulated sugar (⅓–½ c)

100ml vegetable oil

50ml natural yogurt

200ml milk

1 tablespoon butter, melted

175–200g blueberries (1⅓ c); do not
thaw if frozen

Optional Streusel Topping:

2 tablespoons plain white flour

2 tablespoons light brown soft sugar

1 tablespoon white granulated sugar

1 tablespoon butter, not melted

1 Preheat the oven to 190°C (375°F), Gas Mark 5, fan oven 170°C. Prepare the muffin pan.

2 Prepare streusel topping: Combine with a pastry blender (or your fingers) until the mixture resembles fine crumbs.

3 In a large bowl, sift together flour, baking powder, and salt.

4 In another bowl, beat egg briskly with a fork. Stir well after each addition: sugar, oil, yogurt, milk, and butter.

5 When the oven is ready, pour wet mixture into dry. Using a metal spoon, mix lightly just until combined and no dry flour is visible, about 20 seconds. Do not over stir.

6 For best distribution of berries, use the following method. Put a spoonful of batter into each cup to cover the base. Distribute half the berries. Fold remaining berries into the batter in the bowl. Spoon out this batter and sprinkle with either streusel topping or a pinch of sugar. Bake about 20–22 minutes until lightly browned. Frozen fruit might require an extra 2–3 minutes. Makes 12.

Blueberry Variations See pages 66, 75, 102, and 112.

A classic with
a new twist

Deliciously moreish

Blueberry Cheesecake Muffins

275g plain white flour (see page 128)

2¼ teaspoons baking powder

¼ teaspoon salt

1 egg, medium or large

75–100g white granulated sugar (⅓–½ c)

100ml vegetable oil

200ml milk

1 tablespoon water

1 tablespoon lemon juice, at final mixing

Filling:

125g cream cheese or ricotta

2 tablespoons white granulated sugar

125g blueberries (¾ c); do not thaw
   if frozen

1. Preheat the oven to 190°C (375°F), Gas Mark 5, fan oven 170°C. Prepare the muffin pan.

2. Prepare filling: combine cheese and 2 tablespoons sugar. Keep the blueberries separate.

3. In a large bowl, sift together flour, baking powder, and salt.

4. In a medium-sized bowl, beat egg briskly with a fork. Stir in sugar, oil, milk, and water. Prepare lemon juice but do not add until the final mixing.

5. When the oven is ready, add lemon juice to the wet mixture and then immediately pour wet into dry. With a metal spoon, mix lightly just until combined and no dry flour is visible, about 20 seconds. Do not over stir.

6. Put a spoonful of batter into each muffin cup to cover the base. Distribute filling and berries. Top with remaining batter and sprinkle with a pinch of sugar if desired. Bake about 20–22 minutes until lightly browned. Frozen fruit might require an extra 2–3 minutes. Makes 12.

Butternut Squash Muffins

275g plain white flour (see page 128)

1¼ teaspoons baking powder

½ teaspoon bicarbonate of soda

¼ teaspoon salt

2 teaspoons ground cinnamon

¼–½ teaspoon ground cloves

1 egg, medium or large

85–100g white granulated sugar (⅓–½ c)

125ml vegetable oil

50ml natural yogurt

50ml milk

1 tablespoon water

200g butternut squash purée, or
   tinned pumpkin (¾ c)

Optional: 50g chopped walnuts (⅓ c)

Cream Cheese Icing (see page 79)

1 Peel and pulp a small squash. Cut into chunks and put in a saucepan with enough boiling water to cover. Simmer 20–30 minutes until tender. Drain well. Spread chunks on a baking sheet and allow to cool completely until moisture has evaporated. Mash and measure 200g (¾ c).

2 Preheat the oven to 190°C (375°F), Gas Mark 5, fan oven 170°C. Prepare the muffin pan.

3 In a large bowl, sift together flour, baking powder, bicarbonate of soda, salt, and spices.

4 In another bowl, beat egg with a fork. Stir well after each addition: sugar, oil, yogurt, milk, water, and purée.

5 When the oven is ready, pour wet mixture into dry. (Add nuts if using.) With a metal spoon, mix lightly just until combined and no dry flour is visible, about 20–30 seconds. This batter is thick. Do not over mix.

6 Spoon batter into cups. Bake about 20–22 minutes until done. Makes 12. Spread cooled muffins with icing, if using.

Tinned pumpkin is a simple substitute

Moist and lightly spiced

Carrot Pineapple Muffins

250g plain white flour (see page 128)

1½ teaspoons baking powder

½ teaspoon bicarbonate of soda

¼ teaspoon salt

2½ teaspoons ground cinnamon

¼ teaspoon ground nutmeg

¼ teaspoon ground cloves

1 egg, medium or large

75–100g white granulated sugar (⅓–½ c)

125ml vegetable oil

100ml milk

200g finely grated carrot (1 c)

150g pineapple, chopped (⅔ c)*

Cream Cheese Icing:

50g full fat cream cheese

1 tablespoon soft butter (not melted)

100g sifted icing sugar (¾ c)

1. Preheat the oven to 190°C (375°F), Gas Mark 5, fan oven 170°C. Prepare the muffin pan.

2. Prepare carrots. Fine grating is necessary for carrot juice to be released into the batter during baking.

3. In a large bowl, sift together flour, baking powder, bicarbonate of soda, salt, and spices.

4. In a medium-sized bowl, beat egg briskly with a fork. Add sugar, oil, milk, carrot, and pineapple.

5. When the oven is ready, pour wet mixture into dry. Mix lightly with a metal spoon just until combined and no dry flour is visible, about 20 seconds. This batter is quite thick.

6. Spoon into muffin cups and bake about 20–22 minutes until lightly browned. Makes 12.

7. Stir icing together until smooth. Spread on cooled muffins.

Pineapple can be omitted if preferred. Substitute 2 tablespoons orange juice or milk. This will make 10 muffins.

Gingerbread Apple Muffins

250g plain white flour (see page 128)

2½ teaspoons baking powder

¼ teaspoon salt

2 teaspoons ground ginger

1 teaspoon ground cinnamon

¼ teaspoon ground nutmeg

1 egg, medium or large

75–100g light brown soft sugar (⅓–½ c)

100ml vegetable oil

2 tablespoons treacle or light molasses

50ml milk

250ml applesauce (see adjacent)

Optional: 75g raisins or sultanas (½ c)

1 Preheat the oven to 190°C (375°F), Gas Mark 5, fan oven 170°C. Prepare the muffin pan.

2 Peel and thinly slice 2 medium sweet eating apples into a saucepan. Add 200ml water, cover, and bring to the boil. Reduce heat and simmer about 5–8 minutes until the apple has softened. Mash well to make a wet lumpy purée. Cool and measure 250ml for the recipe. Note: Tart cooking apples such as Bramley are not suitable as they create excessive bubbling, causing the muffins to rise quickly and then sink.

3 In a large bowl, sift together flour, baking powder, bicarbonate of soda, salt, and spices.

4 In another bowl, beat egg with a fork. Add and stir well: sugar, oil, treacle, milk, cooled applesauce, and raisins.

5 When the oven is ready, pour wet mixture into dry. Using a metal spoon, mix just until combined and no dry flour is visible, about 20 seconds. Do not beat or over stir.

6 Fill cups nearly full. Bake about 20–22 minutes. Makes 12. Delicious served warm with sweetened applesauce and cream.

Photo: page 60, right

Lemon Muffins

275g plain white flour (see page 128)

2¼ teaspoons baking powder

¼ teaspoon salt

1 egg, medium or large

75–100g white granulated sugar (⅓–½ c)

1 tablespoon finely grated lemon zest
  (2–3 lemons)

100ml vegetable oil

200ml milk

2 tablespoons butter, melted

1 tablespoon lemon juice, at final mixing

Lemon Glaze:

60g sifted icing sugar (½ c)

¼ teaspoon finely grated lemon zest

2 teaspoons lemon juice

1 Preheat the oven to 190°C (375°F), Gas Mark 5, fan oven 170°C. Prepare the muffin pan.

2 In a large bowl, sift together flour, baking powder, and salt. (Add poppy seeds if using.)

3 In another bowl, beat egg with a fork. Stir in sugar, zest, oil, milk, and butter. (Add raisins or cranberries if using.) Prepare lemon juice but do not add until the final mixing. The aim is to give a boost of citric acid without curdling the milk.

4 When the oven is ready, add lemon juice to the wet mixture and immediately pour wet into dry. With a metal spoon, mix lightly just until combined and no dry flour is visible, about 20 seconds. Do not beat or over stir.

5 Spoon immediately into muffin cups. Bake about 20–22 minutes until lightly browned. Stir glaze ingredients together until smooth and spread thinly over hot tops. Makes 12.

Lemon Raisin Muffins Add 50g raisins or sultanas (⅓ c).
Lemon Cranberry Muffins Add 100g chopped cranberries (1 c).
Lemon Poppy Seed Muffins Add 1 tablespoon poppy seeds.

Photo: page 60, bottom

Lemon Cheesecake Muffins

275g plain white flour (see page 128)

2¼ teaspoons baking powder

¼ teaspoon salt

1 egg, medium or large

75–100g white granulated sugar (⅓–½ c)

100ml vegetable oil

2 teaspoons finely grated lemon zest

200ml milk

2 tablespoons water or milk

1 tablespoon lemon juice, at final mixing

Filling:

150g full fat cream cheese

2 tablespoons white granulated sugar

½ teaspoon finely grated lemon zest

1 Preheat the oven to 190°C (375°F), Gas Mark 5, fan oven 170°C. Prepare the muffin pan.

2 Stir the filling ingredients together until smooth. Set aside.

3 In a large bowl, sift together flour, baking powder, and salt.

4 In a medium-sized bowl, beat egg briskly with a fork. Add sugar, oil, zest, milk, and water. Prepare lemon juice but do not add until the final mixing.

5 When the oven is ready, add lemon juice to the wet mixture and immediately pour wet into dry. With a metal spoon, mix lightly just until combined and no dry flour is visible, about 20 seconds. Do not over stir.

6 Put a spoonful of batter into each cup to cover the base. Add a generous teaspoon of filling, and top with remaining batter. Bake about 20–22 minutes until lightly browned. Makes 12.

Light and luscious

Use three lemons for these little gems

Lemon-Filled Muffins

275g plain white flour (see page 128)

2¼ teaspoons baking powder

¼ teaspoon salt

1 egg, medium or large

60g white granulated sugar (¼ c)

100ml vegetable oil

2 teaspoons finely grated lemon zest

200ml milk

2 tablespoons water or milk

1 tablespoon lemon juice, at final mixing

Lemon Filling:

100ml cold water

4 teaspoons cornflour (cornstarch)

50g white granulated sugar (¼ c)

1 teaspoon finely grated lemon zest

3 tablespoons lemon juice

1 tablespoon butter

1   Prepare the filling at least 1 hour in advance so it has time to set. (If the filling is warm, it will spill out of the muffins during baking.) Put the cold water and cornflour in a small saucepan, and stir until cornflour dissolves. Add the rest of the filling ingredients. Stir constantly over low heat until thickened and translucent, about 2 minutes. Transfer to a bowl and put in the fridge to cool and set.

2   Preheat the oven to 190°C (375°F), Gas Mark 5, fan oven 170°C. Prepare the muffin pan.

3   In a large bowl, sift together flour, baking powder, and salt.

4   In a medium-sized bowl, beat egg briskly with a fork. Add sugar, oil, 2 teaspoons zest, milk, and water. Prepare 1 tablespoon lemon juice but do not add until the final mixing.

5   When the oven is ready, add lemon juice to the wet mixture, and immediately pour wet into dry. With a metal spoon, mix lightly just until combined, about 20 seconds. Do not beat or over stir.

6   Put a spoonful of batter into each cup to cover the base. Add a generous teaspoon of filling, and finish with remaining batter. Bake 20–22 minutes until golden. Makes 12.

Mango Muffins

275g plain white flour (see page 128)

1¼ teaspoons baking powder

½ teaspoon bicarbonate of soda

¼ teaspoon salt

1 egg, medium or large

75–100g white granulated sugar (⅓–½ c)

100ml vegetable oil

100ml milk

2 tablespoons water

200g fresh mango, chopped or coarsely grated (1 c)

50g dried mango, chopped (⅓ c)

100ml fresh orange juice, at final mixing

Optional topping: desiccated coconut

1 Preheat the oven to 190°C (375°F), Gas Mark 5, fan oven 170°C. Prepare the muffin pan.

2 In a large bowl, sift together flour, baking powder, bicarbonate of soda, and salt.

3 In a medium-sized bowl, beat egg briskly with a fork. Add sugar, oil, milk, water, fresh mango, and dried mango. Prepare orange juice but do not add until the final mixing.

4 When the oven is ready, add orange juice to the wet mixture and then immediately pour wet into dry. With a metal spoon, mix lightly just until combined and no dry flour is visible, about 20 seconds. Do not beat or over stir.

5 Fill cups nearly full. Sprinkle tops with coconut if desired. Bake about 20–22 minutes until lightly browned. Makes 12.

A delicious duo of
dried and fresh mango

Double orange for
double flavour

Orange Muffins

275g plain white flour (see page 128)

1¼ teaspoons baking powder

½ teaspoon bicarbonate of soda

¼ teaspoon salt

1 egg, medium or large

75–100g white granulated sugar (⅓–½ c)

1 tablespoon finely grated orange zest
   (of 3 firm juice oranges)

100ml vegetable oil

100ml milk

1 tablespoon butter, melted

100ml fresh orange juice, at final mixing

150g tinned mandarin orange segments,
   drained and sliced in thirds (⅔ c)*

*Tinned mandarin segments are sweeter
and less fibrous than fresh. If you prefer
to omit them, substitute 3 tablespoons
milk or juice.*

1   Preheat the oven to 190°C (375°F), Gas Mark 5, fan oven 170°C.
Prepare the muffin pan.

2   In a large bowl, sift together flour, baking powder, bicarbonate
of soda, and salt.

3   In a medium-sized bowl, beat egg briskly with a fork. Stir in
sugar, zest, oil, milk, and butter. (Add dates if using.) Prepare
orange juice and mandarin segments but do not add until the
final mixing.

4   When the oven is ready, add juice and mandarins to the wet
mixture. Pour wet into dry, and mix lightly with a metal spoon
just until combined, about 20 seconds.

5   Spoon immediately into cups. Bake about 20–22 minutes until
golden brown. Makes 12.

Orange Glazed Muffins   Combine 60g sifted icing sugar (½ c),
¼ teaspoon finely grated orange zest, and 2 teaspoons orange
juice. Spread thinly over hot tops.

Orange Date Muffins   Pour boiling water over 50g (⅓ c) dried
dates in a bowl. Soak for 5 minutes. Drain and chop.

Orange Apricot Muffins

275g plain white flour (see page 128)

1½ teaspoons baking powder

¼ teaspoon bicarbonate of soda

¼ teaspoon salt

1 egg, medium or large

75–100g white granulated sugar (⅓ –½ c)

100ml vegetable oil

2 teaspoons finely grated orange zest
  (of 2 firm juice oranges)

50ml natural yogurt

150ml milk

150g chopped apricots, fresh or tinned
  (⅔ c)

50ml fresh orange juice, at final mixing

Optional: 50g dark chocolate chips (¼ c)

1   Preheat the oven to 190°C (375°F), Gas Mark 5, fan oven 170°C. Prepare the muffin pan.

2   In a large bowl, sift together flour, baking powder, bicarbonate of soda, and salt. (Add chocolate chips if using.)

3   In a medium-sized bowl, beat egg briskly with a fork. Stir in sugar, oil, zest, yogurt, milk, and apricots. Prepare orange juice but do not add until the final mixing.

4   When the oven has reached the correct temperature, add orange juice to the wet mixture and then immediately pour wet into dry. Mix lightly with a metal spoon just until combined, about 20 seconds. Do not beat or over stir.

5   Spoon into cups. Bake about 20–22 minutes until golden brown. Makes 12.

Sunshine in
a muffin

An enticing blend

Orange Carrot Spice Muffins

275g plain white flour (see page 128)

1½ teaspoons baking powder

½ teaspoon bicarbonate of soda

¼ teaspoon salt

½ teaspoon ground cinnamon

¼ teaspoon ground cloves

¼ teaspoon ground nutmeg

1 egg, medium or large

75–100g white granulated sugar (⅓–½ c)

100ml vegetable oil

1 teaspoon finely grated orange zest

100ml milk

150g carrot, finely grated (¾ c)

100ml fresh orange juice (about 2 oranges),
  at the final mixing

Optional topping:

1–2 tablespoons light brown soft sugar

1 tablespoon butter, melted

50g pecans or walnuts, chopped (⅓ c)

1 Preheat the oven to 190°C (375°F), Gas Mark 5, fan oven 170°C. Prepare the muffin pan.

2 Combine the topping ingredients and set aside.

3 In a large bowl, sift together flour, baking powder, bicarbonate of soda, salt, and spices.

4 In a medium-sized bowl, beat egg briskly with a fork. Stir in sugar, oil, zest, milk, and carrot. Prepare the orange juice but do not add until the final mixing.

5 When the oven is ready, add the orange juice to the wet ingredients and then pour wet into dry. With a metal spoon, mix lightly just until combined and no dry flour is visible, about 20 seconds. Do not over stir.

6 Fill cups nearly full. Distribute topping. Bake about 20–22 minutes until lightly browned. Makes 12.

Peach Muffins

275g plain white flour (see page 128)

1½ teaspoons baking powder

¼ teaspoon bicarbonate of soda

¼ teaspoon salt

1 egg, medium or large

½ teaspoon almond extract *or* cinnamon

75–100g white granulated sugar (⅓–½ c)

100ml vegetable oil

200ml buttermilk*

50ml milk

1 tablespoon water

Fruit Filling:

200–250g ripe peaches or nectarines, thinly sliced (1⅓ c)

1–2 tablespoons white granulated sugar

1 tablespoon butter, melted

*Buttermilk alternative: 100ml yogurt plus 100ml (extra) milk

1 Preheat the oven to 190°C (375°F), Gas Mark 5, fan oven 170°C. Prepare the muffin pan.

2 Prepare the filling: slice fruit thinly and then cut into shorter pieces. Combine 1–2 tablespoons sugar with melted butter. Mix with peaches and set aside.

3 In a large bowl, sift together flour, baking powder, bicarbonate of soda, and salt.

4 In a medium-sized bowl, beat egg briskly with a fork. Add your choice of almond extract or ground cinnamon. Add and stir well: sugar, oil, buttermilk, milk, and water.

5 When the oven is ready, pour wet mixture into dry. Mix lightly with a metal spoon just until combined, about 20 seconds. Do not beat or over stir. Buttermilk batter is thick.

6 Put a spoonful of batter into each cup to cover the base. Distribute the filling, and top with remaining batter. Sprinkle a pinch of sugar over each top if desired. Bake about 20–22 minutes until lightly browned. Makes 12.

A light fruit-filled
buttermilk muffin

Try adding custard for a warming dessert

Pear Ginger Muffins

275g plain white flour (see page 128)

1½ teaspoons baking powder

¼ teaspoon bicarbonate of soda

¼ teaspoon salt

1½ teaspoons ground ginger

1 egg, medium or large

75–100g white granulated sugar (⅓–½ c)

100ml vegetable oil

1 tablespoon runny (or warmed) honey

2 teaspoons grated fresh ginger root
  (optional)

150ml milk

2 tablespoons tinned pear juice*

200g tinned pears, chopped (1 c)

*With fresh pears, use milk or water.

1 Preheat the oven to 190°C (375°F), Gas Mark 5, fan oven 170°C. Prepare the muffin pan.

2 In a large bowl, sift together flour, baking powder, bicarbonate of soda, salt, and ground ginger.

3 In a medium-sized bowl, beat egg briskly with a fork. Stir in sugar, oil, honey, grated ginger, milk, juice, and pears.

4 When the oven is ready, pour wet mixture into dry. Mix lightly with a metal spoon just until combined and no dry flour is visible, about 20 seconds. Do not beat or over stir.

5 Fill cups nearly full. Bake about 20–22 minutes until golden brown. Makes 12.

Pineapple Muffins

275g plain white flour (see page 128)

1½ teaspoons baking powder

¼ teaspoon bicarbonate of soda

¼ teaspoon salt

1 egg, medium or large

75–100g white granulated sugar (⅓–½ c)

100ml vegetable oil

150ml milk

50ml pineapple juice, at final mixing

300g pineapple (8 tinned slices),
   chopped (1¼ c)

Optional topping: desiccated coconut

1 Preheat the oven to 190°C (375°F), Gas Mark 5, fan oven 170°C. Prepare the muffin pan.

2 In a large bowl, sift together flour, baking powder, bicarbonate of soda, and salt.

3 In a medium-sized bowl, beat egg briskly with a fork. Stir in sugar, oil, and milk. Reserve 50ml tinned juice and prepare the pineapple but do not add them until the final mixing.

4 When the oven is ready, add fruit and juice to the wet mixture, and then immediately pour wet into dry. Mix lightly with a metal spoon just until combined and no dry flour is visible, about 20 seconds.

5 Fill cups nearly full. Sprinkle generously with coconut. Bake about 20–22 minutes until lightly browned. Makes 12.

Delicious simplicity

Bursting with fruit,
topped with crumble

Plum Orange Muffins

275g plain white flour (see page 128)

1½ teaspoons baking powder

½ teaspoon bicarbonate of soda

¼ teaspoon salt

¼ teaspoon ground cinnamon

1 egg, medium or large

75–100g white granulated sugar (⅓–½ c)

100ml vegetable oil

1 teaspoon finely grated orange zest

100ml milk

200g diced ripe plums (1 c)

100ml fresh orange juice (2 large oranges), at final mixing

Optional Crumble Topping:

50g rolled oats (½ c)

1–2 tablespoons soft brown sugar

25g (2 tablespoons) butter, melted

1 Preheat the oven to 190°C (375°F), Gas Mark 5, fan oven 170°C. Prepare the muffin pan.

2 Prepare the topping if using, and set aside.

3 In a large bowl, sift together flour, baking powder, bicarbonate of soda, salt, and cinnamon.

4 In a medium-sized bowl, beat egg briskly with a fork. Stir in sugar, oil, zest, milk, and plums. Prepare orange juice but do not add until the final mixing.

5 When the oven is ready, add orange juice to the wet mixture and then immediately pour wet into dry. With a metal spoon, mix lightly just until combined, about 20 seconds. This batter is quite thick.

6 Fill cups nearly full. Distribute topping. Bake about 20–22 minutes until lightly browned. Makes 12.

Raspberry Lemon Muffins

275g plain white flour (see page 128)

2¼ teaspoons baking powder

¼ teaspoon salt

1 egg, medium or large

75–100g white granulated sugar (⅓–½ c)

100ml vegetable oil

1 teaspoon finely grated lemon zest

200ml milk

1 tablespoon butter, melted

1 tablespoon lemon juice, at final mixing

150g raspberries, quartered (1 c);
  do not thaw if frozen

Topping: 4 raspberries, finely chopped

Optional Lemon Glaze:

60g sifted icing sugar (½ c)

¼ teaspoon finely grated lemon zest

2 teaspoons lemon juice

1   Preheat the oven to 190°C (375°F), Gas Mark 5, fan oven 170°C. Prepare the muffin pan.

2   In a large bowl, sift together flour, baking powder, and salt.

3   In a medium-sized bowl, beat egg briskly with a fork. Stir in sugar, oil, zest, milk, and butter. Prepare lemon juice and berries but do not add them yet.

4   When the oven is ready, add lemon juice to the wet mixture, and then immediately pour wet into dry. With a metal spoon, mix lightly just until combined and no dry flour is visible, about 20 seconds.

5   Put a spoonful of batter into each cup to cover the base. Distribute 150g berries evenly. Spoon out remaining batter and top with raspberry seeds. Bake about 20–22 minutes until lightly browned. Frozen fruit might require an extra 2–3 minutes. Stir glaze ingredients together until smooth, and spread thinly over hot tops. Makes 12.

Blueberry Lemon Muffins   Replace raspberries with blueberries but do not cut the berries.

Zesty intensity

A fresh take on
a modern classic

Raspberry and White Chocolate Muffins

275g plain white flour (see page 128)

2¼ teaspoons baking powder

¼ teaspoon salt

100g white chocolate, chopped (½ c)

1 egg, medium or large

75–100g white granulated sugar (⅓–½ c)

100ml vegetable oil

200ml milk

50ml natural yogurt; or 60g finely
chopped red apple (⅓ c)

100g raspberries, quartered (¾ c);
do not thaw if frozen

Topping: 10 raspberries, quartered

1 Preheat the oven to 190°C (375°F), Gas Mark 5, fan oven 170°C. Prepare the muffin pan.

2 In a large bowl, sift together flour, baking powder, and salt. Add white chocolate.

3 In another bowl, beat egg briskly with a fork. Add sugar, oil, milk, and yogurt (or apple). Prepare the berries in two separate piles but do not add them to the batter.

4 When the oven is ready, pour wet mixture into dry. With a metal spoon, mix lightly just until combined, about 20 seconds. Do not beat or over stir. This batter is thick.

5 Put a spoonful of batter into each cup to cover the base. Distribute 100g raspberries and finish with remaining batter. Top with raspberry pieces. Bake about 20–22 minutes until lightly browned. Frozen fruit might require an extra 2–3 minutes. Makes 12.

Rhubarb Almond Muffins

275g plain white flour (see page 128)

1½ teaspoons baking powder

¼ teaspoon bicarbonate of soda

¼ teaspoon salt

1 egg, medium or large

75–100g white granulated sugar (⅓–½ c)

75ml vegetable oil

1 teaspoon almond extract

150ml sour cream (cultured)

100ml milk

2 tablespoons water

200g rhubarb, chopped (1⅓ c)*

Topping: 50g chopped or flaked
   almonds (⅓ c)

*For frozen rhubarb, thaw just enough
for chopping.*

1   Preheat the oven to 190°C (375°F), Gas Mark 5, fan oven 170°C. Prepare the muffin pan.

2   In a large bowl, sift together flour, baking powder, bicarbonate of soda, and salt.

3   In a medium-sized bowl, beat egg briskly with a fork. Stir in sugar, oil, almond extract, sour cream, milk, water, and rhubarb.

4   When the oven is ready, pour wet mixture into dry. With a metal spoon, mix lightly just until combined, about 20 seconds. Do not beat or over stir. This batter is thick.

5   Fill cups nearly full. Sprinkle with almonds. Bake about 20–22 minutes until lightly browned. Frozen fruit might require an extra 2–3 minutes. Makes 12.

A delectable
sour cream muffin

A blissful blend

Strawberry Rhubarb Muffins

275g plain white flour (see page 128)

2¼ teaspoons baking powder

¼ teaspoon salt

1 egg, medium or large

75–100g white granulated sugar (⅓–½ c)

100ml vegetable oil

½ teaspoon finely grated lemon zest

200ml milk

1 tablespoon lemon juice, at final mixing

Fruit Filling:

150g rhubarb, chopped (1¼ c)

150g strawberries, chopped (1 c)

2 tablespoons white granulated sugar

1½ teaspoons cornflour (cornstarch)

2 tablespoons cold water

1 tablespoon butter

1 Make the filling at least 30 minutes in advance to allow for cooling. Place rhubarb and strawberries in a small saucepan with sugar, cornflour, and water. Stir constantly over low heat for about 3 minutes until juices are released and thickened. Stir in butter. Transfer to a bowl and cool in the fridge.

2 Preheat the oven to 190°C (375°F), Gas Mark 5, fan oven 170°C. Prepare the muffin pan.

3 In a large bowl, sift together flour, baking powder, and salt.

4 In a medium-sized bowl, beat egg briskly with a fork. Stir in sugar, oil, zest, and milk. Prepare the lemon juice but do not add until the final mixing.

5 When the oven is ready, add lemon juice to the wet mixture and then pour wet into dry. With a metal spoon, mix lightly just until combined, about 20 seconds. Do not over stir.

6 Put a spoonful of batter into each cup to cover the base. Distribute filling, and finish with remaining batter. Sprinkle with a pinch of sugar if desired. Bake about 20–22 minutes until golden brown. Makes 12.

Bran

Apricot Blueberry Bran

Orange Date Bran

Sultana Bran

Yogurt Bran

Apricot Blueberry Bran Muffins

275g plain white flour (see page 128)

1½ teaspoons baking powder

¼ teaspoon bicarbonate of soda

¼ teaspoon salt

1 egg, medium or large

75–100g white granulated sugar (⅓–½ c)

100ml vegetable oil

200ml buttermilk*

100ml milk

25g wheat bran (½ c)

100g chopped apricots, fresh or tinned (½ c)

100g blueberries (⅔ c); do not thaw
   frozen berries

*Buttermilk alternative: 100ml yogurt plus
100ml (extra) milk*

1　Preheat the oven to 190°C (375°F), Gas Mark 5, fan oven 170°C. Prepare the muffin pan.

2　In a large bowl, sift together flour, baking powder, bicarbonate of soda, and salt.

3　In a medium-sized bowl, beat egg briskly with a fork. Stir in sugar, oil, buttermilk, milk, bran, and apricots.

4　When the oven is ready, pour wet mixture into dry. With a metal spoon, mix lightly just until combined, about 20 seconds. Gently fold berries into the batter. This batter is quite thick.

5　Fill cups nearly full. Bake about 20–22 minutes until lightly browned. Frozen fruit might require an extra 2–3 minutes. Makes 12. Serve with butter if desired.

Blueberry Bran Muffins Replace apricots with blueberries.

Light, wholesome,
and fruity

Orange Date Bran Muffins

250g plain white flour (see page 128)

1½ teaspoons baking powder

½ teaspoon bicarbonate of soda

¼ teaspoon salt

1 egg, medium or large

75–100g light brown soft sugar (⅓–½ c)

100ml vegetable oil

1 teaspoon finely grated orange zest

25g wheat bran (½ c)

4 tablespoons wheat germ*

250ml milk

1 tablespoon water

150g dried dates, chopped (1 c)

50ml fresh orange juice

If wheat germ is unavailable, increase wheat bran to 50g (1 cup) total.

1　Preheat the oven to 190°C (375°F), Gas Mark 5, fan oven 170°C. Prepare the muffin pan.

2　Pour boiling water over dates in a bowl and allow to soak for 5 minutes. Drain and chop.

3　In a large bowl, sift together flour, baking powder, bicarbonate of soda, and salt.

4　In a medium-sized bowl, beat egg briskly with a fork. Add sugar, oil, zest, bran, wheat germ, milk, water, dates, and orange juice.

5　When the oven is ready, pour wet mixture into dry. With a metal spoon, mix lightly just until combined and no dry flour is visible, about 20 seconds. Do not beat or over stir.

6　Fill cups nearly full. Bake about 20–22 minutes until lightly browned. Makes 12. Serve with butter if desired.

Photo: page 110, left

Sultana Bran Muffins

250g plain white flour (see page 128)

2½ teaspoons baking powder

¼ teaspoon salt

1 egg, medium or large

2 tablespoons light brown soft sugar

50–75g white granulated sugar (¼–⅓ c)

2 tablespoons honey, treacle, or
  light molasses

100ml vegetable oil

300ml milk

1 tablespoon water

50g natural wheat bran (1 c)

75g sultanas or raisins (½ c)

1 Preheat the oven to 190°C (375°F), Gas Mark 5, fan oven 170°C. Prepare the muffin pan.

2 In a large bowl, sift together flour, baking powder, and salt.

3 In a medium-sized bowl, beat egg briskly with a fork. Stir well after each addition: brown and white sugar, honey, oil, milk, water, bran, and sultanas.

4 When the oven is ready, pour wet mixture into dry. With a metal spoon, mix lightly just until combined and no dry flour is visible, about 20 seconds. Do not over stir.

5 Spoon into muffin cups. Bake about 20–22 minutes until lightly browned. Makes 12. Serve with butter if desired.

Great for breakfast or snack

Yogurt Bran Muffins

250g plain white flour (see page 128)

1½ teaspoons baking powder

¼ teaspoon bicarbonate of soda

¼ teaspoon salt

1 egg, medium or large

75–100g light brown soft sugar (⅓–½ c)

100ml vegetable oil

150ml natural yogurt

250ml milk

50g wheat bran (1 c)

75g raisins, sultanas, or dried
   cranberries (½ c)

1 Preheat the oven to 190°C (375°F), Gas Mark 5, fan oven 170°C. Prepare the muffin pan.

2 In a large bowl, sift together flour, baking powder, bicarbonate of soda, and salt.

3 In a medium-sized bowl, beat egg briskly with a fork. Stir well after each addition: sugar, oil, yogurt, milk, bran, and dried fruit.

4 When the oven is ready, pour wet mixture into dry. With a metal spoon, mix lightly just until combined and no dry flour is visible, about 20 seconds. Do not beat or over stir.

5 Fill cups nearly full. Bake about 20–22 minutes until lightly browned. Makes 12. Serve with butter if desired.

Savoury

Apple and Cheese
Cheddar Cheese
Feta and Leek
Gruyère and Onion

Apple Cheese Muffins

275g plain white flour (see page 128)

2½ teaspoons baking powder

¼ teaspoon salt

100g smoked Cheddar,* grated (1 c)

1 egg, medium or large

1–2 tablespoons white granulated sugar

100ml vegetable oil

200ml milk

1 tablespoon water

100g sweet apple, chopped or grated (⅔ c)

Topping: extra cheese

*Or mature Cheddar.

1   Preheat the oven to 190°C (375°F), Gas Mark 5, fan oven 170°C. Prepare the muffin pan.

2   In a large bowl, sift together flour, baking powder, and salt. Add cheese.

3   In a medium-sized bowl, beat egg briskly with a fork. Stir in sugar, oil, milk, water, and apple.

4   When the oven is ready, pour wet mixture into dry. With a metal spoon, mix lightly just until combined and no dry flour is visible, about 20 seconds. This batter is thick.

5   Spoon into muffin cups. Sprinkle with extra cheese. Bake about 20–22 minutes until golden brown. Makes 12. Use a knife if necessary to release them from their paper cases.

Perfect for a
savoury snack

Simple and satisfying

Cheddar Cheese Muffins

275g plain white flour (see page 128)

1½ teaspoons baking powder

¼ teaspoon bicarbonate of soda

¼ teaspoon salt

100g mature Cheddar, grated (1 c)

1 egg, medium or large

1–2 tablespoons white granulated sugar

100ml vegetable oil

100ml natural yogurt

200ml milk

1 tablespoon water

3 tablespoons finely chopped chives
   or spring onion

Topping: extra cheese

1 Preheat the oven to 190°C (375°F), Gas Mark 5, fan oven 170°C. Prepare the muffin pan.

2 In a large bowl, sift together flour, baking powder, bicarbonate of soda, and salt. Add cheese.

3 In a medium-sized bowl, beat egg briskly with a fork. Add sugar, oil, yogurt, milk, water, and chives.

4 When the oven is ready, pour wet mixture into dry. Mix lightly with a metal spoon just until combined and no dry flour is visible, about 20 seconds. Do not over stir. This batter is thick.

5 Spoon into muffin cups. Sprinkle with extra cheese. Bake about 20–22 minutes until golden brown. Makes 12. Best served warm. Use a knife if necessary to release them from their cases.

Feta and Leek Muffins

275g plain white flour (see page 128)

2 teaspoons baking powder

¼ teaspoon bicarbonate of soda

¼ teaspoon salt

1 egg, medium or large

1–2 tablespoons white granulated sugar

75ml vegetable oil

250ml milk

1 tablespoon water

200g chopped leeks (2 c)

2–3 tablespoons oil for sautéing leeks

100g feta cheese, rinsed and chopped (¾ c)

Optional: 40g pine nuts (¼ c)

Topping: extra cheese or pine nuts

1 Preheat the oven to 190°C (375°F), Gas Mark 5, fan oven 170°C. Prepare the muffin pan.

2 Sauté leeks in 2–3 tablespoons oil over low heat for about 5 minutes, stirring frequently until soft but not browned. If using pine nuts, spread them on a baking sheet and roast in a preheated oven for 1 minute. Do not scorch.

3 In a large bowl, sift together flour, baking powder, bicarbonate of soda, and salt. (Add pine nuts if using.)

4 In a separate bowl, beat egg briskly with a fork. Stir in sugar, oil, milk, water, sautéed leeks, and feta.

5 When the oven is ready, pour wet mixture into dry. Mix lightly with a metal spoon just until combined, about 20 seconds. Do not over stir. This batter is thick.

6 Spoon into muffin cups. Sprinkle with topping. Bake about 20–22 minutes until lightly browned. Makes 12. Best served warm. Use a knife if necessary to release them from their paper cases.

Photo: page 118, right

Gruyère and Onion Muffins

275g plain white flour (see page 128)

2 teaspoons baking powder

¼ teaspoon bicarbonate of soda

¼ teaspoon salt

100g Gruyère,* coarsely grated (1 c)

1 egg, medium or large

1–2 tablespoons white granulated sugar

75ml vegetable oil

250ml milk

1 tablespoon water

3 medium white onions, sliced thinly

2–3 tablespoons oil for sautéing onions

Topping: extra cheese

*Other hard cheeses can be used, such as Cheddar.

1   Preheat the oven to 190°C (375°F), Gas Mark 5, fan oven 170°C. Prepare the muffin pan.

2   Sauté onions in 2–3 tablespoons oil over low heat about 10 minutes, until soft and golden. Stir frequently to prevent scorching. Allow to cool.

3   In a large bowl, sift together flour, baking powder, bicarbonate of soda, and salt. Add cheese.

4   In a medium-sized bowl, beat egg briskly with a fork. Add sugar, 75ml oil, milk, water, and sautéed onions.

5   When the oven is ready, pour wet mixture into dry. Using a metal spoon, mix lightly just until combined and no dry flour is visible, about 20 seconds. This batter is thick.

6   Spoon into muffin cups. Sprinkle tops with extra cheese. Bake about 20–22 minutes until golden brown. Makes 12. Best served warm. Use a knife if necessary to release them from their cases.

THE BASIC MUFFIN

Because of its simplicity, the basic muffin benefits from a little added butter which enhances both flavour and texture. In addition, by slightly increasing the acidity of the batter with yogurt, apple, or lemon juice, the rising gets an extra boost. If you are looking for a plain buttermilk muffin, you can use the recipe on page 32, and omit the filling. The basic muffin can be enjoyed plain or with jam, or even a little chocolate icing for a treat! Remember that baking is about chemistry and each ingredient has a role to play. To learn more about this, see page 12.

275g plain white flour (see page 128)

2¼ teaspoons baking powder

¼ teaspoon salt

1 egg, medium or large

75–100g white granulated sugar (⅓–½ c)

100ml vegetable oil

50ml yogurt; or 60g sweet apple, chopped (⅓ c); or 1 tablespoon lemon juice added at the final mixing*

200ml milk

25g butter, melted (2 tablespoons)

*Alternatively, you can use 1 tablespoon extra milk.

1   Preheat the oven to 190°C (375°F), Gas Mark 5, fan oven 170°C. Prepare the muffin pan.

2   In a large bowl, sift together flour, baking powder, and salt.

3   In a medium-sized bowl, beat egg briskly with a fork. Stir in sugar, oil, yogurt/apple, milk, and butter.

4   When the oven is ready, pour wet mixture into dry. (Add lemon juice if using.) With a metal spoon, mix lightly just until combined, about 20 seconds. Do not beat or over stir.

5   Spoon batter into muffin cups. Bake about 20–22 minutes until risen and lightly browned. Makes 12.

GLUTEN- AND WHEAT-FREE BAKING

The terms 'gluten-free' and 'wheat- free' are often confused. A person diagnosed with coeliac disease is unable to eat any foods containing gluten, including wheat, oats, barley, and rye, while someone who is wheat intolerant might be able to include other grains in their diet. On their own, non-wheat flours produce a dense powdery texture that practically dissolves in the mouth, leaving nothing to chew. By combining some of these flours, there is a marked improvement which can be enhanced further by adding extra egg. For top quality gluten-free baking, a special ingredient called xanthan gum is needed to give that tender chewiness that makes baked goods so enjoyable to eat. Xanthan gum is a natural product commonly used as a thickener.

Ready-mixed gluten-free flours are now widely available. For best results, use gluten-free *white plain* flour. (Brown is not suitable, and self-raising flour loses effectiveness with storage.) Adjust as follows:

• add 1¼ teaspoons xanthan gum to the dry ingredients

• use 2 medium eggs

• add 1–2 tablespoons extra liquid

Note: With British gluten-free self-raising flour, xanthan gum should be reduced to 1 teaspoon, as there is already a small amount in the flour mix. With self-raising flour, omit baking powder but do not omit bicarbonate of soda or salt. Other countries may differ.

Some final tips: When converting to gluten-free, I would advise writing out the revised list of ingredients before starting, to prevent errors. Secondly, gluten-free batter is very different from wheat flour batter so you will need to disregard the usual light mixing technique which is used for inhibiting gluten development. Instead, without gluten, gluten-free batter needs to be thickened with xanthan gum, and this process requires a good stirring (not beating) for about 20 seconds until the batter is well mixed and starting to thicken. Gluten-free batter will look smoother than regular muffin batter. Without adequate xanthan gum and stirring, the batter will be too wet and the final rising and texture will be poor.

SUGAR AND FLOUR NOTES

Please also refer to page 12.

Most of the recipes in this book specify 75–100g sugar which is 1¼–1¾ level teaspoons per muffin. I would recommend starting with 85g until you find your preferred level of sweetness.

When measuring sugar by volume: 75g sugar is a level ⅓ cup, 85g sugar is a rounded ⅓ cup, 95g sugar is a heaped ⅓ cup, and 100g sugar is a level ½ cup.

For sugar-restricted diets, the sugar can be reduced to your desired level. For example, 2 tablespoons of sugar will be equivalent to ½ teaspoon per muffin. A reduction in sugar will also have an effect on texture, so it is best not to omit it completely. Low sugar muffins are best served warm.

This book calls for British plain (cake) flour. Self-raising flour is not recommended as its raising agents become less effective with prolonged storage. However, if you would like to use self-raising flour, omit the baking powder from the recipe but do not omit bicarbonate of soda or salt. (In America, self-raising flour contains salt, but not in the UK.)

For Canadian all-purpose flour, increase the liquid by about 2 tablespoons. American all-purpose flour is variable from state to state so you may or may not need to increase the amount of liquid.

In other countries, check the protein content of your flour if possible. British cake flour has 8–10g protein per 100g, while bread flour has 12.5–13.5g per 100g. If your flour has a protein content similar to bread flour, you should increase the liquid by 1–2 tablespoons.

For best results in baking, scales are recommended. Measuring flour by cups is imprecise and can result in batter that is too wet or dry. If scales are not available, please measure your flour as follows: over a plate, heap flour into the measuring cup, give several taps and jiggles to settle the flour, and then level off.

CUP MEASURES FOR FLOUR
(1 cup = 240ml)

Weight	Volume
275g	2 c (shaken down)
250g	1¾ c + 1 tablespoon
225g	1½ c + 2 tablespoons